ANARCHY
EXPLAINED TO
CHILDREN

ANARCHY

EXPLAINED TO

CHILDREN

José Antonio Emmanuel

TRANSLATED BY **NAFTA**

ILLUSTRATED BY **Fábrica de Estampas**

EDITED BY **Piu Martínez**

SEVEN STORIES PRESS

New York • Oakland • London

Originally published as *La anarquía explicada a los niños* by
the International Anarchist Library, Barcelona, 1931.

TRIANGLE SQUARE
BOOKS FOR YOUNG READERS

SEVEN STORIES PRESS
140 Watts Street
New York, NY 10013
www.sevenstories.com

LIBRARY OF CONGRESS CATALOGING-IN-PUBLICATION DATA
is on file.

ISBN: 978-1-64421-449-7 (paperback)
ISBN: 978-1-64421-450-4 (ebook)

College professors and high school and middle school teachers
may order free examination copies of Seven Stories Press titles.
Visit https://www.sevenstories.com/pg/resources-academics
or email academic@sevenstories.com.

PRINTED IN CHINA

9 8 7 6 5 4 3 2 1

Contents

To the children of the Spanish proletariat.

Feeble and small are children,
for that very reason, sacred . . .
—ÉLISÉE RECLUS

NBP*

This pamphlet answers a question several comrades have posed to us: How will we educate our children? Our response follows the dictates of reason and science.

Dedicated to the children of the Spanish proletariat, we hope these humbly composed pages will orient their learning towards true renovation.

We ask their parents and teachers to disseminate healthy doctrines at home and in school by banishing all fanaticism and aspiring to liberate the youth of the nefarious oppression exercised against them.

Many share the blame for how education has stagnated in a haggard state of servitude, from which it must be redeemed and consoled.

May these brief pages be stimulating to all.

—EDITORIAL GROUP, 1931**

---

* Though "NBP" may be an acronym for "Note en Bas de Page" (i.e. "footnote" in French), this note was formatted as a foreword in the 1931 Spanish-language edition published by the International Anarchist Library (IAL).

** This note was co-authored by the editors of IAL, which José Antonio Emmanuel founded.

1

What Is Anarchy?

Anarchy, dear children, is the doctrine that refuses to conform to the organization imposed upon humanity since the creation of society and, instead, tries to constitute a life based on the sacred principles of universal love and human solidarity.

Its mission is to bring an end to the prevailing inequality that divides people into poor and rich, exploited and exploiters, enslaved and enslavers. For life to be as it should one must defend the free manifestation of our faculties, the spontaneity of our actions, and total liberation.

Anarchy seeks to destroy the causes that are harmful and detrimental to the free development of the individual and the collective, and I define these below. Never forget that in fighting them, we are working for the well-being of all.

Militarism

Militarism is the armed force used by those who have taken over life in order to impose their injustices and solidify their evils. This force does not recede even in the face of crime; it arms people against each other and pits them against those, like you, like your parents, like your siblings, who have made a virtue of work. When we rebel against this mode of conduct, when we rise up against those that commit injustices against us, they crack down on us. Not content with seeing us oppressed, they provoke wars, they decimate humanity, and their crimes pile up along the path.

Anarchy opposes this brutal force with peace. The anarchist dreads war, is opposed to war and longs for peace, because peace is the fundamental point of their lifesaving doctrine. They consider all beings kin. They do not want us to be separated by borders, but instead brought together by a shared love: the total and absolute emancipation of all. The weapons of anarchism are the book, labor, and the word. With these they combat the organized force of militarism, and with these they will triumph over the butchers and devourers of humanity. With the book, with labor, with the word, they call upon everyone, making them see that, over brute force, these give rise to an idea whose ultimate triumph is indisputable.

Clericalism

Clericalism is the farce with which the usurpers of life have surrounded themselves to demonstrate that their impositions, their tyrannies, and their oppressions are just and agreeable with a "god" they have forged so as to clothe their acts in kindness. With this god, they guide the hearts of "believers" and, amidst the outlandish splendor and luxury of the temples they have erected, they craft orations and prayers to convince everyone that they are the directors and organizers of life, and that society constitutes a fall into sin that does not follow the mandates of this god, the tyrannical orders of this god. Above all, clericalism takes hold of you, dear children, to intimidate you with the fantastic torments of an inferno and the pleasures of a heaven you must earn by submitting yourselves to the representatives of this god on earth. Those that do not become their followers, those that distance themselves and rebel against them, they declare "enemies" and oppose with the power of their god, the omnipotence of their god. They create the "devil," which tempts humanity, all of us, and condemn us to eternal pain and an infinite fire.

To secure their dominion over all beings, the clerics call for help from the military, which has organized life into armies poised to make their divine principle triumph. Anarchy employs science to oppose this overarching, absolute power, this terrorizing potency. Science, which is the organized knowledge of life, discovers the law that governs worlds and societies; it reveals everything attributed to god, innate to god, to be false and erroneous; this singular natural law, which overthrows divine law, destroys divine omnipotence, is the natural law of human progress. By virtue of this progress, one arrives easily at the contemplation of life in all its purity; that the earth is not the dwelling of god, nor the temple of god; that the human being is not of divine origin, but that we appeared on the earth by virtue of slingshots and incessant evolutionary transformations in the animal organism until arriving at our species; that the end of the world is not subject to the providential destinies of god, but that science fixes its goal by a rational mode and in agreement with natural laws.

Anarchy destroys religions because they are absolutist, despotic, cruel, and bloody. And it seeks to protect you from these, dear children, so that you can rebel against the terror of being condemned, the fear of being punished, the pleasure of being rewarded. Punishment and reward exist in bourgeois society because they were created by the clergy and the military. There is only one recompense: that of fulfilling one's duty to life, of being useful to your fellow beings, and of contributing to the introduction of the new society where no hate exists, nor resentment, nor classes, nor vanities, nor tyrannies.

Capitalism

Capitalism is society organized by the criteria of brutal and inhumane egoism, wherein one class retains absolute power over another. The latter produces and works, while the former takes advantage of common efforts to create riches and privileges without which it could not survive. Capitalism erects a self-sustaining power, establishes states, divides people into nations; its tentacles dig into the entrails of the earth to steal the money that it monopolizes and distributes unequally; it penetrates into every domain, from the workshop and the factory to the total hoarding of lives and land, it dictates laws and imposes them to grow stronger and consolidate itself; absolute lord of existences, capitalism does not hesitate to denaturalize work, appropriating production, regularizing life on the basis of usurpation and violence. Master and lord of the social organism, capitalism upholds *clericalism* because it aids in its nefarious designs and counts on *militarism* because it sustains itself and serves it as support. Its *law* is respected and obeyed by all because capitalism is enforced by assassins and senators. Capitalism calls this its "mandate"; it names this "power."

But Anarchy, dear children, rises up against this manner of conceiving and organizing existence. Anarchy aspires to eliminate all causes that plunge humanity into the lethargy of opiates. It has no use for states that, by their very fact of existence, bring about irritant inequalities and bloody injustices. Against money, Anarchy proposes the free circulation of products; against well-paid jobs for the privileged, it proposes work distributed to each according to their abilities; against the insane egoism of the powerful, it proposes the needs of each are met according to the needs of all; against oppressive laws, it proposes the law of love; against egoism, it proposes the idea that the land belongs to those who work it and produce.

This is Anarchy, beloved children. This, and much more that I am unable to explain to you in these brief pages, but that time will teach you and, through it, life will reveal to you.

Anarchy wants you to investigate the origin of all these inequalities, the reason for all these injustices, in preparation for comprehending that the life you lead, a reflection of your parents' bitter existence, should be otherwise, cannot remain as it is. Life is beauty; life is justice; life is peace and well-being.

Anarchy puts you on the path toward achieving and obtaining a good life; and, since you are the weakest, the most innocent of this ill-fated organization, you ought to know how to rebel against all that oppresses and imprisons you. You are not alone. Among us are those who fight to free you of the bitterness surrounding you, to free you from the brambles tearing at your flesh, from the poisons coursing through your pure and sacred hearts.

We will not offer you temples, nor make you worship divinities, nor fill your soul with fear, nor corrupt your consciences by muddying them with fraud and deception.

Lift your eyes: look around you. The time for healthy joys, happiness, and peace is on its way.

Anarchy accelerates the arrival of this hour, this joy, this happiness, this peace not yet before you.

2

How to Reach Anarchy?

There is a path that leads toward Anarchy, dear children. You are guided along it by the school, the union, and the athenaeum.* We will explain these three powerful forces which you will be able to rely on for the rest of your lives.

School

You will understand right away that we are not talking about the reactionary bourgeois school that, until now, you have been forced to attend. We offer you an alternative that is not based on foolish, inane teachings, but on the *school of rationalism*.

You ought to know that our school has a scientific foundation, which is what should guide your lives. Your teacher, perhaps the only person whose attempts to educate you are deserving of your gratitude, defines this school as one that supports the spontaneous development of your faculties,

---

* The anarchist athenaeum was a community center providing social services and leisure activities for working-class urban dwellers. Funded and run by workers in their spare time, this institution provided access to cultural empowerment and educational services which were meant to foster class solidarity and a spirit of political agitation. Their programming sought to foster intergenerational militancy for the anarchist cause.

a place for the unfettered pursuit of your physical, intellectual, and moral needs.

I am talking about Francisco Ferrer. Study his life, follow his work, make him your apostle and your guide. We are indebted to him for creating the rationalist school in Spain, an act that honored humanity. He banished from school the three farces I mentioned before: militarism, clericalism, and capitalism. Thanks to him, the children he educated had science permeate their brains and reason infiltrate their hearts. He sanctified your right to broaden your minds and educate yourselves beyond dumpy old schools and their shriveled up teachers. He banished the idea of divinity from your minds and replaced it with the cult of justice and goodness. He opened the prison of ideas to turn it into a pleasant and delightful place. He saw in you what humanity must see in you: the seed of a new humanity.

Honor Ferrer by following his doctrines of redemption. Ferrer was an anarchist; that is, he struggled against the powerful clerical, militarist, and capitalist forces that turn society into formless, disgraceful chaos. You must learn to struggle as he did. Get acquainted with this redemptive doctrine and, through you, the new world we are building together will emerge.

It is time you learn that if you do not set yourselves free in school, it will be difficult to liberate yourselves when you grow up. Emancipation must begin with you. So that is why Anarchy gives you an education. May your teachers also be imbued with this highest truth. If not, you will be left to your own meager devices and it will be your fault when you fall into the arms of life's slave drivers.

School should teach you to be rebels, to defy this corrupt, disgraced society. The enemies of your parents, of your siblings, are and will be your own enemies. The cause of your unrest and bitterness also weighs on those who gave you life and who live alongside you. You must join us in this holy struggle. The eradication of our pain and unhappiness depends entirely on you.

We do not want you to be resigned; resignation is for the bourgeois teachers and the prison-schools they rule over.

Anarchy offers a school of freedom. There are three books that will help you achieve liberation. Three books that have educated three generations. Three books that should always have a place in your schools, as guides and anchors of your lives: *The Universal Pain*, *The Conquest of Bread*, and *The History of a Mountain*. Their authors, three lights who still shine brightly, are, respectively: Sébastien Faure, Peter Kropotkin, and Élisée Reclus. Do not forget these titles and names. By the time you are twelve, they must have a place on the shelves of the library you will keep expanding. They will make known to you the root causes of your sufferings, the origins of your enslavement in work, the seeds of life and existence, the history of the earth. In them, you will learn to overcome the difficulties of struggle; you will find the strength to resist and hope in what is to come. Let these books be the first steps you take in life: a precious walking stick for your progress.

The Union

When you leave school, Anarchy will not abandon you. As you grow, as you advance—right now, you are young—it will compel you to continue the struggle, increasing your rebellion. Anarchy taught you to open your eyes and see the world. It made you see inequality. It showed you where egoism dwells, where evil lies, where our eternal enemy hides. Anarchy showed all this to you, it compelled you to be vigilant so you could prepare to combat and defeat the forces it has revealed to you.

Once you have reached this point, the doors of another organization will open: the union. If, in your childhood, you had one school, in your youth you will not lack another: the school of the proletariat.

The same enemies that surrounded you as children surround you now. An organization based on struggle is required, a home where you can take refuge and recover your faith, revitalize your ideals, and increase the strength you must build up a hundredfold to wage the final, decisive battle. The same anguish, the same bitterness that besieged you as children, besieges you as men. Enter into it; take shelter in it. All of us united, all identified with one another, we will resist better. Be faithful and show solidarity to your comrades, your brothers in struggle and rebellion.

Do not abandon this new school—the school of life. Together with your parents, continue fighting for a better world.

The Athenaeum

So that you lose neither faith nor enthusiasm in this titanic struggle, Anarchy offers you a third space where the struggle for culture is practiced: they are the libertarian athenaeums, counterparts of the unions, guides of the unions, leaders of the militants.

It is not only the struggle for material improvement that should unite us; the struggle for culture should bring us together, too. Those longings for knowledge you first had at school? You must continue expanding, magnifying, intensifying them here.

You see, then, how Anarchy watches over you, dearest children.

3

How Do We Make Ourselves Worthy of Anarchy?

To identify with Anarchy, to dignify your lives, you must fulfill these anarchist postulates.

1

HELP

Never disengage from those who fight like you, those who suffer like you. In school, you had them by your side. Now, they are with you in the workshop, in the factory, in the mines, still thirsty for justice. Wherever you see your siblings, help them. Reach over the frontiers erected by privilege to offer a hand to those who are victims of today's bourgeois society.

2

Support

Whoever hesitates, inspire them with courage; whoever despairs of seeing triumph so out of reach, give them strength. Mutual aid is a sacred and universal duty.

3

EMULATE BEAUTY

Do not imitate that which is perishable and ephemeral. Dispel and drive away all sources of harm: they remain the inheritance of human imperfection to which we are chained. Lift your gaze to the beauty of life, which lies above this chaos of ignominy.

4

Labor

Everything in nature is a form of labor, which it is your mission, to the extent of your capacities, to perfect. Do not resign yourself to being the machine's serf or the muscle's slave. Dignify your labor, make it beautiful, purify it.

STUDY

5

STUDY

Let books be your companions, your counsels, your guides. We will never know enough. Whoever adds science, adds Anarchy. Investigate by yourself, reveal the mysteries that surround you. Instruct and educate yourself. This is the only inheritance you must leave behind in life.

6

Love

Science places no stones in the heart. A pure and humane love deepens in us. No matter how far away they are, how distant they find themselves, every being is loved by us.

7

Protect

They who care plenty, help plenty. Protect the weak. To the elder, the sick, we are united by even more love because they are feeble. That poor, old person you see, was as strong as you, as brave as you; that disabled person is also like you. Think that you can be like them; think that bourgeois work will age and sicken you. Protect them! Think about those who are not with us: the imprisoned; because they fought, because they defended us, they have no freedom. Remember them!

8

CULTIVATE

The earth is your mother. The fields are your sustenance. If we cultivate them, we will harvest ripe fruits and fine crops. Leave no land sterile. Give the earth the care it needs to feed you and keep you alive. In the ideal world, sow ideas, scatter thoughts, write, and act. In the real world, let the seed fall in soil that, if well fertilized and tilled, will nourish the seed so it grows into a plant that blossoms and bears fruit.

9

Own no slaves

Aspire to be free and for the cravings of your freedom to embrace everyone. Enslave no one. No living being can be imprisoned with impunity. Open the doors of all cages, file the bars of every jail, where—like the caged bird—human beings suffer and endure. Be liberated and liberate, with you, everyone else. Open the doors of your heart so that all vices can exit it, all the defects that managed to get in. Be free and be pure: own no slaves and turn not into one.

10

Work and fight, Anarchy tells you. They told you: work and pray. Leave prayer behind. There is only one prayer you must never forget: the prayer of work. Work for the well-being of humanity, for the end of suffering, for the final departure of bitterness. Rejoice in a free humanity.

This is Anarchy, dear children.
Blessed you will be,
if you understand and practice it!

Enact, then, your vision
for a new life of purity
and kindness.

—JOSÉ ANTONIO EMMANUEL

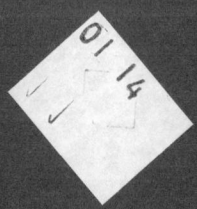

With influences ranging from Rousseau to Godwin, the illustrator, without forgetting the ideas of Proudhon, Bakunin, and Kropotkin or the revolutionary practice of pedagogues such as Pestalozzi and Ferrer, libertarian education has evolved and has adapted to different social contexts, convinced of its fundamental role in achieving a more just and free society.

The literacy of the popular classes, the education in gender equality, and the anti-authoritarianism practice are some of the revindications of the anarchist movement accomplished by the educational reforms of the Second Spanish Republic. For the first time, children from families without economical resources were able to attend school. Decisive advancements towards this aim have been contributed by editors, militants, and pedagogues such as José Antonio Emmanuel, founder of the press International Anarchist Library (IAL), and author and editor of this pamphlet; Antonia Maymón, anarchist and feminist pedagogue, tenacious defender of the education of children in a single school without class or gender distinctions; or

---

* This note corresponds to the 2020 Spanish-language edition published by Libros del Zorro Rojo.

Félix Carrasquer Launed, founder of the Rationalist School Élisée Reclus, a free and self-managed educational center.

The establishment of the Second Spanish Republic in 1931 marked, furthermore, the beginning of a period in which anarchist ideology became increasingly influential, a consequence of the political and labor force of this movement. Within the program of pedagogical transformation proposed by anarchism, the school—which, according to Ferrer, is the most efficient medium to attain the complete, moral, and intellectual emancipation of the working class—embodied the foundation of a new society. Anarchist education would develop not only inside classrooms, but also in different institutions linked to the pedagogical traditions of the labor movement: teaching reforms initiated the creation of the first popular and school libraries, the anarchist athenaeums, and popular universities. These centers of working-class culture, authentic hubs of literacy and reading promotion, focused on teaching adults how to read and fostering reading habits in childhood. Such skills allowed the popular classes to emancipate themselves from obscurantism and ignorance, and to transform themselves into the conscientiously free and equal actors of a new society.

—PIU MARTÍNEZ, 2020

Translating this book required negotiating a central, and perhaps unresolvable, tension: proximity to the source text and adherence to the author's aims. As scholars and poets, our approach to translation has tended to lean more in the former direction than the latter, but we hope that this rendition of the text into English will be useful to young people today who wish to learn about the ideas and history of anarchism and leftist politics. In light of that hope, we have made the language of our rendition more contemporary and fluid (in certain places) than a literal translation would have required. We have also updated some terms in accordance with shifts in the politics of language, such as rejecting "man" as a stand in for humanity and shifting from "masters and slaves" to "enslavers and enslaved." Moreover, Spanish grammar tends to permit more complex syntactic statements with greater ease than English typically affords. We have thus streamlined for readability where necessary, while also attempting to retain an overall sense of the rhetorical complexity that makes Emmanuel's source text so animated and pedagogical and thus, memorable.

Nonetheless, this translation does not constitute the total rewriting of the book that would be necessary to update it for our era—nor would we wish to do so. Certain historical elements, such as the athenaeums, are unfamiliar in our current moment of neoliberal mass culture and austerity regimes, though similar forms of collective organization and grassroots organizations continue to fulfill similar roles. Above all, however, we value the idea that children can understand complex ideas and issues with far greater lucidity than contemporary educational institutions suggest. There are moments of rhetorical excess, technical jargon, and historical references in this book that we could have translated into plainer language, but we trust that young people, perhaps in conversation with the adults in their lives, will be able to understand these textured passages—at least as well as we have understood them ourselves. After all, the original book contained those elements and was written with the same audience in mind. In this spirit, parents, teachers, librarians, adults in general: we invite you to think of yourselves as translators when engaging with this book alongside younger readers.

We hope that this book is the beginning of a conversation between children, between adults, and between children and adults. As it was in 1930s Spain, as it is now everywhere, the fostering of intergenerational solidarity remains crucial against the threat of fascism and neoliberalism. We learn best when we learn together. May this learning guide us in the construction of more just worlds and futures.

—NAFTA, 2025

José Antonio Emmanuel was one of the many aliases of José Ruíz Rodríguez, an educator, philanthropist, and anarchist from Málaga, Spain. Until 1923, when Primo de Rivera's dictatorship began, Ruíz Rodríguez went by Max Bembo. Under this pen name, he authored *La mala vida en Barcelona: Anormalidad, miseria y vicio*. In the early 1930s, after the proclamation of the Second Spanish Republic, he reappeared as José Antonio Emmanuel. As Emmanuel, he collaborated with the International Committee of Schools in promoting nontraditional schools. He also founded the IAL Press, whose International Library Collection published affordable, brief works that explained concepts such as the proletariat's organization, union action, and anarchy. During the Spanish Civil War, Ruíz Rodríguez vanished without a trace, and it is not known what happened to him. As a political activist and innovator who never lost sight of those most in need, especially children, he holds a special place in the history of Spanish education.

NAFTA (North American Free Translation Agreement / No America Fraught Translation Argument), ratified in 2019, is a collective of three poets writing from the occupied territories of

Canada, Mexico, and the United States. They have translated *Commonplace / Lo común* by Hugo García Manríquez, *String Theory* by Karen Villeda, and selections drawn from *Poelectrons* by Jesús Arellano.

Piu Martínez has edited *Anarquía explicada a los niños*, *Cartilla Escolar Antifascista*, and *Gato en el camino*, among other works, and is director of Libros Asombrosos, a collection published by Barrett.

Fábrica de Estampas is an Argentine graphic collective founded by Delfina Estrada and Victoria Volpini. They create original posters and prints employing etching, woodcut, linoleum, and monocopy techniques. They also offer printmaking courses. Fábrica de Estampas uses engraving, an intrinsically communal practice, as a tool for community building.